POET FIRE

POET FIRE

DIMENSIONS OF A MIND ON FIRE

TERRELL W. SIMS

CITI OF
BOOKS

CITIOFBOOKS, INC.
3736 Eubank NE Suite A1
Albuquerque, NM 87111-3579
www.citiofbooks.com
Hotline: 1 (877) 389-2759
Fax: 1 (505) 930-7244

Ordering Information:
Quantity sales. Special discounts are available on quantity purchases by corporations, associations, and others. For details, contact the publisher at the address above.

Printed in the United States of America.

ISBN-13:   Softcover   979-8-89391-559-4

Library of Congress Control Number: 2025903502

Contents

At Night

At night while lying in bed in the darkness
Cloaked under the veil of the blackness within the room
I'm a prisoner within my own mind
Captured in my thoughts,
yet adorned with illuminations and imaginations
And being lost in the mediation of my mind,
While looking upwards,
Communicating with the stars in the heavens
And seeing the stars baffled but uninterrupted
As they form an alliance in the skies
And the darkness overcomes me with overwhelming fright
Clouding my path of sight in the pasty moonlight
When the stars are bright and the moons in flight
And the darkness comes before the dawn
But the moon reflects the sun's light for the light at night
But when the sun sets the darkness becomes the night
And seeing the animations of the stars
As they appears into the reality of space and time
Shining beautifully and brightly
Burning with illumination and fire in the blood moonlight
Fervently falling across the dark and velvety black skies
A manifestation confined by limitations of my mind

Romance

Romance is a metaphor
A primal storm of emotions
A maneuver of the heart
An aphrodisiac of the mind
When you are next to me
your sweat perfumes your body
Oh so titillating to the touch and feel so inviting
Your kiss so wet, so warm, so romantic
As it fills my body from head to toe with lust
Your touch puts me into a dream state
I see aromas, I hear colors
I fall further into a valley of romance
Like a meteor falling to the earth
waiting to express itself on impact

Beloved

Your eyes are like a moon light summer eve
Warm and reflective, like the rays from the Sun
Reflected off the surface of the moon
I love every inch of your body piece by piece
As it beautifully captures the moon's effervescent radiance
Through the night
Night is day and day is night,
capturing the moon lights beauty, into flight
Your voice is like a heartbeat warm and tender,
Liken to a sweet smelling savor
The vibrations of your voice like a medley of melodies
I desire your radiant love do not deny my love for you
My expression of love is poetic
and my heart beats a melody of love

The Ocean

During the night fall as the moon
and the stars come into focus
My mind takes me on a journey of imagination
And seeing the ocean gleaming
As the moon light is reflected off the ocean's surface
The ocean is corporal with many things to see
The vastness and the magnificence of its glory
The significant power of its roar
The majesty and the architecture of its design
And the excellence of its waves
And the beauty of its vibrant blue currents
Crashing upon the sandy brown shores
The ocean whispers and speaks
as its groaning on the surface
Moving and breathing yet a quiet storm
Underneath then finally calming its violent rage

In My Mind

As the sun sets I see shadows in my mind
I see the moon's trajectory in rotation
and the given forces of its orbits
And the sun's sphere of intense heats
and pressures and illuminating fires
In my mind
I see the atmosphere and the cosmos
and touching the universe
All in my mind...
I travel in my mind, I see places from afar, as the stars fall...
When the sun sets
My heart beats like the creatures move in the night
I see shadows and ideas in abstract in my mind
I think in terms of types and metaphors, facsimiles
and hyperboles
Being present in my mind, running rapidly
and continuously in my mind
Like the universe the deep, the dark,
the depth is there
Present in my mind

Alone

Loneliness echoes around me
while feeling the vibrations of
Every molecule and defying
every element of space and time
I sense the physical realm with effort
using my emotions as my guide
Allowing that my shadow is cast
During daylight hours and seeing the things
not in the physical realm
As my mind moves in thought it takes me
to another realm or state of mind
Being all alone

A True Reflection

She cries a romantic cry of satisfaction
Certainly it exhibits her beautiful body
As a gallery in a beautiful garden of art for my eyes
Her charms are my dreams
Become nightmares of necessity
and thoughts of the rainbows
Portrayed as exotic sculptured beauties
Laying within the fold of colors and shapes,
faded fantasies
I need not say one word
But fill you up with my eyes to attract you
I'll tell you things as gemstones for your ears
And images on the surface of the sea reflect imagery
As we reciprocate sexy illusions together
And the tones in my mind ring truth and reflections of you

Reality of the Soul

What does the rationale of my heart declare,
About the issues afflicting the condition of my mind?
Captured in my thoughts and held hostage there
My mind is like melodies
Formed and fashioned by the tune strings of my heart
With deep deliberation and unfathomable deep footing
What foundation has my heart established for me?
What path or epic journey shall I take?
Then suddenly life fades away
Like a puff of smoke ascending into the heavens
Life is a vision or a dream broadcast for all to see
My heart doth sway for it is not solid
My heart is the key to my mind,
it unlocks the door to my soul
The soul of a man is likened to a big city
Being visited and traveled for all to see

A Poem Came to Life

Through much deliberation
And connecting of continuous intersecting lines
Of geometric equations called fractals
A poem came to life which started as an inspiration
And kindled into flame
The words of which ascends off the pages
In empty particles in space
and collisions of forces in time
To see you laugh and smile is the created
organic expression of poetry
Growing within my heart
And putting it into passions longing for words to say
As desires solemnly fade into the pass
But the spoken words lives on forever

During the Night

As the night passes by I began feeling her body next to mine
The soft caress of smooth tight skin against the velvety silk sheets
Flowing so effortlessly over our bare skin body's
And as fire runs through our fleshly anatomy's like electricity
When moving becomes current transferred from body to body
In streaming romantic declarations
You're a glass of wine bubbly
and fragrant and sweet to the taste
Swirling though every taste bud
And terminating every thought
as we perform our expressions of love
And as two worlds collide
We are lost in the ecstasy of our minds

Thoughts and Reflections

Poetry is a very powerful organic instrument
Spoken through a flowing garden of words
Tasting the flavor of every word and phrase
And creating the essence of life
through spoken word

Dimensions of a Broken Mind

Miles traveled across the seas
Excavating the broken dimensions of my mind
And salvaging my emotions
And when arriving in the far reaches of my mind
And inducing the allure of invisible magnetisms
And places I've never been before
Partaking of an abyss of the new wine
And channeling the knowledge of quantum controls
In unwritten laws and unseen forces
Inciting the elicit glean to quicken endorphins
And annotated enzymes by making the unseen
Seen in visions and dreams
Like turning coal into diamonds
or liquid form into solid matter

Audible Sound

Caught by the imagery of fiery places
a consciousness perceived with pain
Counting the seconds and measuring the moments
And emerging in a universal sound
Out into the atmosphere in deviating unilateral codes
And strange energy forms resonating in electrical alignments
While the spinning earth rings
like a bell in high frequencies
And mysteries untold
Vibrational resistance and erratic productions
Of symmetrical interferences revolve with the bowels of the earth
Sound frequencies and harmonic module assimilations
Balancing the spinning earth
Like a house with no doors confer
with dimensions of acoustic sounds

Altered States

Android compilations derived from
Robotic and metaphysical managements
Traveling into deep emotional levels
Beneath hypnotic codes in parallel dimensions
Higher energies transferred into living cells
Catapult across boundaries
set in nature's homogenous life forms
Anthropomorphic energies condensed is matter stabilizing
And astrological alignments grasping support
In different altered states because energetic implications
Change particle friction charges as they exist
The vast energy components of the interstellar space
And vacuums exploit the time travel continuum
and black rift anomalies
Within the paradigm shift core
of the Milky Way galaxy

Sheeple or People

Lies fading into dissimulating deceptions
Magnifying and falsifying human thoughts
And distortive sights of view
Embellishing instinctual hominoids
and other carbon based organisms
In human beings, poison configurations,
non-metallic in nature
And chemical by products, in side effects
Masses being brainwashed sheeple
Modification of manifestations of an evil mind
Colorful false images stupor with abominations
Blinding and coupling broken people
Leading them under a false guise
of pretentious circumstances
Leading cattle into slaughter

The New World Order

Broad basins, disc-like flying objects filling the skies
Dynamic polymorphous compounds
And compelling assiduous vitalizing vapors
Creating erosive microorganism throughout the skies
Mutations in the earth's atmospheres
With prevalent earthquake phenomena in diverse places
Phantom dimensional deity's coming out of the shadows
And radio signals connecting wavelength patterns
Controlled from remote places
Dark perpetual images in the minds of the people
Forming negative analytical algorithms nation wide

A Romantic Tale

Pouring the wine, she trembles
Always she hot before the intimacy
Cupid's infallible arrow has pierced her misty heart
Shedding every silent tear drop falling
How must she be feeling, as I?
Shall we fear the lechery of our burning desires?
Or the hunger within the fires?
Rubbing the back of her neck with my hands
Running my fingers through her soft porous hair
Kissing her with my hand behind her head for the support of a kiss
The cold flush of her heart sends warm feelings
Through every orifice of her body
Making love to her, I'll do it slow
Then she'll loosen up her mind and do it freely
Sliding her dress down slowly over her hips
Laying down and closing her eyes
I'll come to her with a red rose
And with the stem in my hand,
I'll slide a beautiful red rose from the top of her forehead
Across her firm lips and all the way between her breast
Then in the same manner, I'll kiss it and I'll lick it
For the taste of the rose petals
And the triggers that satisfy the essence in my mind
And through my striking loins,
expand the notions of the love making
Ever so raving in my mind

A Mind on Drugs

Cutting roots for the connections
to the other side of reality
Through dimensional ports arriving places
on dark long-gated vivid planes
Stretched out through many ongoing dimensions
Perceived to be a thought but actually there in reality
Driven by propelled forces of addictions
A mind traveler binging on psychedelic trips
Contrasting kinetic images, shapes shifting beings
And on the dissension back to the third dimension
Eyes glazed over passing through an open door
In the fabric of time, hosting invisible invaders
Coming through unaware of their present with you

A Glass of Wine

Born in Bordeaux
Conforming to any shape
As Rich and Dark as the blackness night
Yet red in color
A captivate essence so nimble,
delicious, and supple
And warming In effect
Therefore bold and broadened but continental
A ripe peach teeming
with sweet organic provocative essence
And yet so light and airy
A slight hint of rose in aroma
An appetite nurturing the flavor and taste
Absolutely seasoning and satisfying
An exquisite temptation
An etiquette and protocol for wetting your palate

Tropical Ocean View

Warm tropical crystal clear blue waters
Organic coral reef system arrangements
Electric eels and manta rays
Immersed free flowing warm rushing
aquatic deep blue waters
Birds soaring through the heavens in flight
Cuttlefish burrowed in amongst the dusty rock formations
And openings in the ocean floor
Camouflaged seaweed throughout the ocean surface
Is flourishing germination from the glowing rays of the sun
Way down below on the mantle of the continental shelf
Monarchs of exotic ocean life and tropical fish
Flow among the crystal blue palaces
And the ocean top mantle view

A Painting of Spring Flowers

A bountiful array and beautiful décor
of a red rose painted canvas
Vividly splashed in velvety violet and blue
Sweet roses and affections painted
early in spring or sweetly spiced herbs
And pollinated flowers perfumed
Violas blooming herbaceous
and blue pedaled clean flowers
Perennial planted roses
in radiant bright colors and strategically planted
Derives constant symmetry's
and continual bouquets and blue flowers

Dance

Dance is a process of animation
Through an optical illusion
within the human unconscious mind
And exposed at will through human bodies
Dance is a physical rendering of brain cells
Interpreting signals into euphoria
And transferring energies into bodily movements
The acceleration of the minds complex assembly model
Accompanied metaphors of dance
And beautiful visual images
and cosmic advance realization of
Creations rhythmic movements
Structures of sound wave communications
of the body's erotic languages
And recognition of quantum mechanics
in intrinsic human forms

The Wonder of Animals

A prologue of creation the beautiful
inherent skins of the animals
Inbred with amazing primal rhythms
Displayed and outlined skins
grafted in permanent ink
Shown through the illustrious
canvas of the lion's skin
Designed from the ancient days
tigers never lose their stripes,
They're perpetually printed!
Animals the personification
of instinctual creatures made magnificent
And naturally an organic beast of burden
The epidermis membrane
of the zebra hide is tame
And textured gracefully
While the turtle with its rock hard exterior
Constitutes a slow moving creature

Feelings

Words flow from my lips like sweet nectar
As the wind blows, whistles and whines
through the aisles of Egypt
And the infidels curdling lips as sweet as candy
Feelings and words produce
deep sensations of a viral confection
A reflex of subjective pleasures
And feelings matching chords and vibrational tones
Created harmonies, not discord
But the sentimental notions of persuasion
Commiserate the confectionery treasures of the heart

The Northern Lights

A world made in the veneer of fantasy
Cultivating affections draw from the deepest well of emotions
Snowfall drifts down from the ambience of the atmosphere
And winters frozen chill appropriates the snowfall during winter
But the aurora of the northern lights produce a continuous flow
Of the solar wind far out into the atmosphere
And the artful array of the rainbows translucent colors
Generates a spectacle within the sky
The blends and fluorescent
gleaming colors show a shadeful portrayal
Of the cosmos and exhibits lights

A Hot Passionate Kiss

As I walk into a room an aura proceeds before me
Impacted greatly by the hysteria of the woman within the room
My emotions and my feelings synthesized become one
To a duplication of propagation and facsimile of the same expression
Cold and calculating I began quenching the flame of my emotion
To no avail, instead gently I pressed my chest against her
Beautiful brown bosoms as we tightly embraced the sweet acidity
And enticing perception Of a French perfume oozes slowly into my nostrils
Gently sliding my hands down the smooth round curvature of her fitly
Framed body and as my hands so erotically moved so gently
Touching her firmly plumped buttocks
Her eyes interlocked with mine and holding on to the
Expressive emotional reflection in her eyes
We kissed passionately
Her soft and tender lips pressed against mine
Her lips were wet and moist and so delicious
The dreamy faction of enthusiasm in her eyes
Induced the rage of infatuation
As I feel the fervor of fire within every passionate kiss

Angelic Tribulations on the Earth

Carbon dioxide is present in the atmosphere of the Earth
Greenhouse gases increased every decade at alarming rates
Heated global warming cause negative natural effects
And destruction upon the Earth
Revelations in the air immobilize
the rulers and authorities, climaxed
Surmounting legions and principalities in the air
CO2 and aerospace imitative coercions usher
In adversities in photosynthesis
Concentrations of CO2 and
atmospheric derivative pressures
And ascending capacity and powers
of compound chemical reactions
Travail against the nations

Mind Control

The human body is a container
Made to contain the source of life
The mouth of a human being is an outlet
To project the vibrations of speech energies
The human body contains two mind forces of energy
The conscious and the unconscious minds
The unconscious mind is the path into the human body
The connection into the conscious mind
Words are invisible yet external
As speaking vain words exudes energies of negativity
So also the positive speaking creates positive issues in life
But brainwashing creates a
negative prism encompassed all around us
Putting us inside other dimensions of darkness
And confusion of a mind control aura

Knowledge in Outer Space

Within the interplanetary
system of deep space globalization
The spirited essence of man
remains exceedingly aloft
And embedded within the
dusty rock surface of the modular ground
The essence of moving through the deep
Labyrinth space of external extremities
Within the margin of sweeping latitudes
Ornately organized and following through black holes
In outer space has increased man's technology
And understanding from stage one manifesto
Into the second system of blackness
And interplanetary orbits and formations

Winter's Frozen Bite

Mountains extend up from the Earth
rising in royal splendor
Flowing effortlessly into the heavens
Caped in polar ice white ridges
And heightened pillars and peaks of expressions.
Snow rumbles down the steep sleek slopes
In pervading avalanches of pristine white snow
And filtering down melting away
rapidly into the ice cold glacier sea
Floating icebergs, massive cores of frozen ice
Filling the frozen winter seas
and large glacier sheets of ice
And deep terrestrial reservoirs
and freezing climates in the seas

The Essence of Spring in a Dream

Beautiful is the day and the amazement
of the Earth's wondrous creations
Of beauty and elegance to the magnitude and power
Of its flourishing rivers and seas
And the bountiful spectrum of lights
Transfigured into spirit and formed into dreams
And the living sentient illusions
in my mind as I close my eyes
In sleep reveals the fanciful
harnessed Utopia of processed energies
And projection relays of colors, shapes
And moving illustrations of animations
Etched in beautiful sky blue cloud scapes
Nestled around the towering Cascade Mountains
A precursor of the quantitative megalithic forest
Outlined in hypnotic giant trees
across plush green landscapes
To the trickling down, percolating streams
of effervescent flowing waters

Words

Words are true and can be the truth
Or a force that binds the mind
Words rise into the atmosphere
and penetrate into the heavens eternal
Particular words are triggers, cause and effects
Carnal knowledge and word configurations
of mind, body and soul
Electrical vibe frequency wave patterns transmitted
And picked up out of the air
Broadcast light or dark energies and misogyny
Words as images come to life in metaphors
And sentence structure realities
Words are eternal sounds echo
out being vibrations bouncing off
And vocalizing fragments and creations of sound
And verbal manipulations abound

Elegant Tulip

An elegant tulip fluted crystal wine glass,
Is the prelude to a kiss
As I'm holding a chilled glass of wine
As I dipped the tip of my finger
into the fine French red wine
And ooh la la! As her lips pressed together gently
Like firm succulent grapes ripened
on a vine or squeezed in a press.
From her mouth the warm wet moisture
dampened my finger
The process of bodily connections
are intertwined within our minds
And interweaved as we cleaved to one another
Sweet smells of almond powder sprinkled herbs
Of bodacious brown blends
and cinnamon spiced aromas filled the air
Subtly I exclaimed,
"Always I miss your beautiful brown eyes"
Until the next time I see you
And if I never see you again,
I'm going to miss you forever

Louisiana Lands

Far over yonda, Louisiana blue deluge
On the brink of the bayou
The blue sky falls upon the swamps
And the deep mired quick sand marshes from afar
Where the waters meet the sky blue heavens
In the full abundance of the day
From the pelican reefs to the albatross call
Far across them fields of the marsh land falls
Far and wide through the meadow tall
Down into the bayou, onto the southern call
In the grassy null terrain
Under the rainy rolling sky, velvety high
As we wonder asunder,
the plunder of the swamp
In the hope of Louisiana lands

The Mind of Illumination

Words are likened to a beautiful,
illustrious craft
Used in portraits and graphic illustrations of design
My thoughts are the strokes
of a masterfully used paint brush
Which painted upon the canvas of my mind
Vividly imagined words inside my head
Of explicit dreams,
deep colored schemes of the unseen
And brushed abstract painted themes
All within a collage of visions and dreams
A manifested successions of imagery
Seen in dreams during a systematic effect of sleep
A cataloged epiphany inside my mind of a portrait
Using words, painted Picassos of poetry
In my mind expressed and articulated
Marvelous rich colored tones
of a gray shaded plateau of dreams
Dreams so strong and with such
strength and image reflection
Protrude outside my mind into the air
Within independent projections of visions
Captured during daylight hours
Casting shadows and conformations
show within the air

Passions

At this time, of space and reality
The ambiance of the evening
Passions deeply fill my heart with emotions
My eyes moistened with tears, filling so deeply
The depths of the deepest ocean
And haven fallen so far within the vanity
Of my mind, as my eyes, fully shut.
And seeing the dreamy passions in my mind
Of exotic plush leopard skins
Laying and aligned from door to door
Slinky, appealing, and dark sultry tones
Set the mood for the evening
Laying naked beside lighted candles
And red rose petals all throughout the floors
So arousing and how inciting, her comely fragranced skin
I came hither to her cuddly essence
Within the cradle of her voluptuous, firm bosoms
Taken over and subdued by an avalanche of erotic feelings
And the essence of exchange.

Flighty feelings soar within my emotions
Dangling at the door of romance
Metaphors of falling dreamy illusions captivate me fully
Fueling the passions, and lighting the fires
Burning within my desires, and stimulating the lust
And exploding the emotional vibe
of colorful, vivid, sexy sounds
So enticing and exotic and enriched
upon every zone of erotic delight
Two hearts setting into motion
The flavor of romantic capsizing sentiments
And animated in the mind, emotion, and will

Forecast

The forecast is a rainy day
Momentous rainfall rapidly moves
Across the cloudy skies
Cloud cover accompanies every rain drop
Falling and beating like a drum
As the rain begins to fall upon
the eerie damp ground
Lucid dark and black expressions
Of gray beaded skies fall upon my chest
My heart beats like a drum to the notes
of the sound of the music
Like torrential rain beating through the trees
Or a momentous shipwreck capsized upon the seas
All around me in a world, forevermore slowly disappearing
And incessantly a changing reflection of an image
Within two different minds occupying the same space

Hot wax

A candles glowing oil and illumination
Are the source of sweet aromas and flame
The vitalizing warmth of a candle light dinner
Or the smell of a candle in flame
From the crown of the candle
to the base of the stand
The quintessence hot fluid glows
Therefore absolutely invigorating
And so exhilarating to the touch
And oh so wet and hot and flowing
The gooing, molten, waxing motion glowing
It runs, oozes, and slowly trickling down
An intoxicating rush.
The site of hot wax glowing,
stimulates her essence flowing
The hot oozing, seeping, circulation
Seductively flowing and waxing down
upon her supple breast
For her sensual, sensitive sensations
Of elastic temptations and tingling silky brown skin
Which the aroma of the candles flame ignites
The burning of her body insane

Climax: A Bubble Bath Experience

A refreshing bubble bath
is the climax of the day for a woman
Relaxing in a smooth antique, marble tub
Delicately soft, foaming mousse
Soothing exotic oils and refined velvety,
organic lathering soapy sensations
And silky massaging smooth gels
rubbed all over her body
So creamy, slippery and wet
A flavorful and fruity scented fragranced perfume
And culminating balm to expedite her senses
Euphoric pinnacle of excitement
In a warm refreshing bubble bath
Releasing her zone of relaxing pleasures
In a frenzy of baby soft skin splashing
As the soft massaging suds caress
every sensitive part of her body
Into spasms of sheer enjoyment
and bubble enticing fortitude
For relaxing, painted nails and pampering servitude
The savory scents of ambrosial orchids
and crowing plush lotions
Slowly massaged apogee into the skin
For titillating excitement and relaxing enjoyment

Hot Brewed Coffee

Steaming hot brewed dark roasted coffee
Vinegary spiced and full bodied
Acidic, sharp and tart
A biting acerbic blend coffee
Hot and porse rolling smoothly down the throat
In a warm descend, subtle, and warming
A vivid, floral note, spicy hot and bitter aftertaste
All throughout your mouth and tongue so hot and steaming
A chocolate colored perfection in dark roasted dreams
A balanced, unique and a pleasant warm essence
For character, distinction, and a spiced hot palette
Fragrant dark brown coffee beans
A grinded brown bean to perfection
And a procured execution and fiery percolation
Like the red hot chili's stinging bite but bitter

The Battle Within

Practical application and a generalization
Of living in a secular core value system
Interpreted through third dimensional sight realities
Life as we know it, being average and subtle
On an ongoing process unaware
And as we roll the proverbial ball
Ending up where it may
Just painfully unaware of the rounded circumference
Of our daily modular circumstances and ruling over it
Lost with the confusion of a purple haze
Reality's dissension laid hold of my life
Bringing me down to the far reaches of a pit
A dark abyss, a foretaste of Hell's negativity in experience
Not imagined by human minds
This I could not afford but grace did
Then ascension propelled me
to the higher heights of joy and happiness
Through and unto the creator of spirits and far away
And gracefully above all secular society
A higher ground ascending into the heavens, Amen.

The Dark Side of the Moon

At night during the moon's reigning
Shine and gaze upon the Earth
The exposing lights reflection
Conceals the dark side of the moon
Because forever this reality of night
There, is always real in my mind
The energy of the moon's reflections
And interfering cerebral waves of gray brain matter
The cause of affected and exuberant
Adrenalized pandemonium's of a slave
A chemically imbalanced manifestation of activities
On different human emotional levels
Energizing the ocean waves and powering forces
Of anomalies and surface moon dimensions of space
The dark side of the moon is the dark side of existence
But the Earth's reflection also shines
On the dark side of the moon
What happens above, also manifest below
In comparison to the Moon and the Earth below

The Kansas Sunflower

The sun is the vein
of life's reality for the Sunflower
The soils intrinsic powerful life
force nourishes the flow
Secretions of sunlight,
photosynthesis, and H2O
Are the essence of existence of life
Up from the vein of the stem, life protrudes
Out from the head of the flower
A honey bee extracts the nectar
The pedals expressive yellowish glow
Exhibits the life of the flower
As the Sunflower bathes within the shining rays
Of the glowing sun, the forecasted yellow flower grows
Its growth is as an orchard of flowers of the field
Shooting and following upward and real
Reaching unto the sun they grow and exclaim
For the choicest flower shines and glows
In a fountain of flowing fields of a garden
Rich expressions of a beautiful flower
And a wondrous array of aromas surround us
For it's the gorgeous,
organic life of the Sunflower

Cosmic Warfare on the Earth

Numbers are the building blocks
Of everything known in existence on the Earth
The latitude is the dividing line
From one end of the Earth to the other
Many different events and structures fall in place
Along the latitude line of existence
Latitude coincides with longitude
Longitude concurs with latitude given
The celestial mathematical equations
In angular formulas and terrestrial mundane equations
Celestial influences and dark angelic forces
Aiming constantly in bombardment of projections
Focusing negative energies on the earth
Cosmic events cause different cellular reactions
In human beings and influence manifestations
And mounting scales of unseen exertions on the Earth
Dark shades of blackness merge
into the twilight gloaming shadows
A mind of a prism of energies apprehended
And interim inducing forces in essence of the mind
Solely dimensionally traveled into the blackness
Of confusion and complacent
Encompassing the body of energy flow

Smoke Narcosts and Colorless Shades Hidden in Plain Sight

Dazed within revolving doors
And evolving spinning wheels
Of a deep, unseen calligraphy of signals
And sign crystallizations of mind
Hidden scripts and un-ripened forbidden fruit
A definitive haze replaced, superseded and supplanted codes
Within the written languages and other modes of communications
A scripted writing system forged in a grid iron niche
Of collective intelligence views to reciprocate patterns
And electrical brain waves and mind metamorphosis in flight
Ring stones of information and automations
Of deceptive fraudulent schemes
So mysteriously not known or understood in real time
Lost in the lying perceptions and false images
Of an animated elixir and negative modes
Of communicative vibrations hidden in plain sight

Music of the Opera

Monolithic rushing waterfalls
Flourishing rich green herbal plant life gardens to fruition
Whistling airy tones of fluttering flutist notes
And harmonizing B-flat scales in unison
And melodic chorus symphonic concerts
Pleasant chords played as light as feathers
And the tranquil music of the opera
And the lyres strumming sounds
The visuals of the profound sounds
Centered heart beats and the breathe of life
Within the music and of the sounds
created images in our minds
Within the bounds of the profound sounds

Clowns

Skinny, fat, frowny, and brown
Short, tall, funny and round
Many in numbers,
make great big sounds
In all some are very small,
and make up for the ones very tall
And in all they constantly trip and they fall
Then in a moment next, he runs into a wall
Running out and over, they trip and they fall
Then over again and again they fall
Bright white, make up face
Horse shoe shaped eyebrows
standing looped and tall
Squeezable soft nose, it blows, it honks
And indeed the lips, a permanent smile
Like a big red bow ribbon in style
Round bald headed,
surround and abound and abase to his face
Besides each ear, hair planted like bushes
Suspended balloon pants, held up tight
Funny little midget car by far
Rubber inflated horn and honking sounds to boot
And speaking of boots or shoes big, red, and floppy
All under a high pitched tent

What So Ever

How can the clay exclaim to the potter?
Shape me this way or that!
A lump of clay typifies the heart of a man
Fashioned by the hands of the potter
The spinning Earth is comparable
To the spinning wheel of the potter,
Moved and navigated left or right,
fast or slow, still or no
A carved sculpture, casted molded
In shapes desired of the potter's design
For the clay cannot shape itself
But the potter, what so ever he desire
And controls in the kingdom of Men

Mind Matters

Brain matter is the essence of reasoning
Through a personification of one self
Between the spheres of the mind
there is the imagination
But the persona is an ever urging
allegorical impulse
Striving in succession of the self
To dig deeper within the center Amina
The very center of man's being
and the actual life essence
A reference to find what is wonderful
Also the heart beats in rapid succession
During illusions and images projected in dreams
And allusions, vividly spoken
and rhythmic intervals in time

Life is Organic

Within the artificial premise of life
The cerebral inauguration of synthetic
And counterfeit life form existence is benign
Digital code and bacterial chromosomes
elude to an attempted endeavor
To poison the natural fruit of life's energy and continuation
Spoken into existence, the universe came into being
Ancient of days is the creator
The selfless sanctity of a primordial process of life
Is contained within the child bearing hips of a woman
Organically life possess sustainability
Blueprinted and balanced organically
within its own natural eco system

The Wonderful Transformation
of the Butterfly

When the caterpillars mutate and change, they shift
Tentatively subsiding animation and livid transformation
States of metamorphosis and processes of life
The cause and motions of an effervescent existence
Take form inside the silky cocoon of its shell
So it all began, demise and the caterpillars end
Sprouting up and shooting out,
Living to unleash its vibrant life form in the air
The caterpillar became the radiant life of the butterfly
Aloft and floating translucent soft wings
and motions caressing the air
Dazzling and naturally harmonic movements flow
Brilliantly harmonized it flutters
and displays a beautifully blended
candy colored array

A Flame of Fire

A blended quality fire of orange and yellow shades
The looming fire crackles glowing,
comprehensively explosive flames
The friction of the heat's conductions
effectively arises within the flame
The luminous fiery countenance domain
reverberates in smoke
The flaming conducive smoking inferno,
the conductivity,
And a fiery flame
The resounding flaming fire
burning and emissions with the flame

Tornadoes

At high altitudes in the air
when hot and cold temperatures mix
Pressurized infrared apocalyptic rotations
increased within the air
The atmospheric tunneling proxy
The effect of super high winds
and generating noisy dynamos
And disastrous tornadic weather
twisting cyclones in the air
High winds and debris solely mix
The movements and destruction
of a catastrophic path in sight
The sounds, winds, sirens and forces
removing oxygen from the air
As time stands still
within the interior core of the storm
The subatomic particles spinning
and topping out in flight within the air

Between Two

The thrust of a slippery slope
Plump, sweet organic walls of affection
Bursting storms of pleasure and oozing emotions
Between two, lust and desire become one in emotions
A ripe peach of passionately infused connections.
An erotic sanctuary, an exotic prism,
served hot and sizzling
A hot fiery bed of roses organically arranged
In a smooth pulsing heartbeat, the prognosis is heat!
Erect with pressure and gradually building up
A dish of steaming hot bubbly loco motion
Exploding the episode and massaging
the erogenous zones
In a pleasurable forte of implosions fulfilled

The Essence of Life

Poetry is a very powerful and organically
a magnetic instrument
Spoken through a flowing garden of words.
Poetry spoken eloquently and colorfully
in many different ways
Is like the suns expressive glow
The fire of the sun is poetry as a sea
of a fiery whirlwind
The bright molten shine
And discharge of expressive
effervescent glowing infernos
And explosive flaming fires to pontificate speaking
Through magnetic demonstrative UV rays
and vibes of flowing fire
The sun's golden ore within its shining rays
Beyond the sunrise of brief passions
In streams of glimmering sunshine beams
And light sparks flickering warm roasted rays
Poetry is incandescent of life
Every word and phrase creates the
essence of life through spoken word

Psychia – ('Trick)

Mental illness by name is many
Many spirits of deep ambiguous low pitch vibrations
And distorting sounds in voices
Speaking to the minds of the people involved
Schizophrenic, manic depressant, psychopathic minds
The names of the spirits, going out among the people
Psych drugs, not a cure, but a temporary fix of a Band-Aid
A placebo to the spiritual
Spell binding drugs are the spells casted
diverting in dimensional travel
Restricting third dimensional sight in other
Realms of controlled environments
In essences psychiatric is a trick
to the psyche and a cure to none
The most high God is the cure in the fight against the
Principality and powers in the air

My Mind at Work

The systematic process of my mind at work
Distinct individual words and codes
systematically lined from end to end
From a mind of essence and in sight
through vision projection,
Broadcast in dreams
In no particular order, never in phrases,
Only individual words that come together systematically
In essence of creation precisely substantiated
developing phrases to sentence structure parades
Viewed in the film banks of my mind from reel to real life
And organized grouping and vital word advocate uttered speech
Rolling down to my tender lips off the storage banks of my mind
To word metaphors in phrases
and sentences of enunciated words
And expressions of poetry
And displayed essence speaking formulas
and mathematical equations through using words

Caught in the Web

At last my love, spring time has come
The budding flower has purpose for the bumble bee
The birds have begun to sing sweet songs to mine ears
As we ascend to new heights in our emotions
So my heart has embraced the warmth of your affections
For you dwell within the beating chambers of my tearing heart
For love has lifted mine eyelids to see, through the veil
Passionately place around my heart
The stronghold have fallen upon me
I'm intertwined into the web of your love

She a Flirt

She smiled franticly,
as I puckered up for a bubbly pneumatic kiss
Smooching emphatically,
tasting the effervescent red wine
from her beautiful, moist lips
And the romantic antics
and foolery of her sexual capers
Elude to flirtatious frolicking gestures
Within the carousing escapades of sexual mischief
Leading to more, than just a romantic kiss

The Fruit of Forbidden Lust

Lust is a quantum transport of dark formations,
In other places through astral projection
Out of time a lustful mind travels through eternal space
Connecting with dark matter, in question, to other places
Lust is the vanity of dimensional places
Falling within the sphere of absorbing
magnetic osmosis, seducing forces
A drawing snare of attractions,
Cerebral lust attracts dark matter
between space, outside of time
Which craving the raw fruit of forbidden lust explores
A device of trespass in immoral codes
Transgressions of natural phenomena and laws of ethics
And vague issues of dissipation manifest

A Love Letter

Lift up your voice and shout
into the vastness of the earth
And the atmosphere
A love letter spoken in written form
Lady, how fair are your comely hips
To speak with your tongue
Within the grasp of your lips
You're a novice and your echo, I ascertain.
With the pencil of my mouth,
I write to you a love letter with my lips
For it is given me to speak
with the lovely organ of my lips
A heavenly harp of suffice which played
From the tune strings of my heart, beautiful strummed
I make sweet love to you, with no touch
By my words I activate your senses erotic flow
If I touch you, the conveyance of my fingers do the hearing
And they listen to all your perceptions
With my words, I shape like clay the images in your mind
I taste the letters through the color of my words
The electricity of my touch and the stimulation
of my ora commands you
I get confirmation from the erotic reaction of your figure flowing
You confirm me with your flesh
And the erotic languages of your mind and body

Modern Romance

Waiting for you, while reading romantic novels
I felt different about you
Born to romance in the mind as if it were the first time
And due to the lack of my conviction
Yet at the magnificence of the dawn
The taste of your lips satisfied me
With you, romance is so easy
And tomorrow comes quickly
For today we must love, as romancing aristocrats
We grow stronger in love, as romancing is forever and today

The Only One

As I stared down her voluptuous stature
Gazing repeatedly at the endearing soft spiral
And free flowing firm locks of golden blonde hair
Her hair in a glance like silk curtains, draped across her breast
A ruby red kiss she planted upon my lips
The taste of passion cherry, all the way down my throat
The warmth of her soft lips, radiates the flowing winds of her passions
For my tears have flown away, never more can be another you,
Nor your lips on another

The Passion Cherry

I picked a beautiful passion colored cherry by the stem
I held it up above her head
Passionately tilting her head backward
And sucking the dark red cherry into her mouth off the stem
As we kissed, we shared the passion
And flavorful sweet cherry between our lips
After blowing the succulent cherry from my mouth,
To her suckling sexual lips, she swallowed
She was wearing a very revealing brassiere
You could see the firm imprints through her sheer precipitous blouse
As the blood began to fill within my lower region
There was a connection in the twinkling of our eyes as they met

A Romantic Evening

Holding hands as we walked along the ocean shore through the sand
Strolling barefoot across the cool soft blades of grass
Cuddling upon beautifully weaved blankets
And long stem roses in array for decor
Sipping red wine in excess and enjoying finely aged cheese,
Along with the aroma of the wine
Speaking poetry and romantic tales to one another
Staring into each other's eyes, for romantic moments,
And the silence before we kiss
Finally, here we are, creating the moments that last
As we live to treasure every feeling, held most dearly from the past

A Romantic Place

Enchanted by the stillness of her mood, under a trance
Interpreting signals and sighing winds of vivification
Looking for the heavens, in the scope of my desire
Loving the taste of her flesh
Perfumed with the sweet aroma of fresh flowers
And the physical signs of arousal, longing and yearning for sexual pleasure
And mutual response, while love making
And how beautiful is the music of romance between two

Summer Air

After winter's cold day, the Summer Skies are beautiful and blue,
Way up high!
But way down below, are illusions of a blue elegant terrace moon at night
The sandy straw blows in the wind
On the fields of the dusky African violet fair
As the lady's slippers become aromatic in the wind,
Floating on the river down stream
And the lotus flower leads to the honeysuckle road
While the chaff blows ill and far
But the sweet tender aromas in the air, conjures hallucinations
Of oleanders and the Lilacs bud, when the iris and the daffodils bloom
So we enjoy the summer days,
Drinking mimosas and the amber champagne
As the tawny rose petals fall onto the ground
Like the beautiful stenciled, tattered lace
This is the lives we share
All within the beauty, and aromas of the summer air

True Love

True love is a romantic masterpiece
Mesmerized from the first time I saw you
I've counted the days
Imagined every moment in time.
Loving you always, never in my mind apart from you
These thoughts are always in my mind
Oh my! I have fallen deep within romantic music
The art, the Mozart of love is so amusing
And moving together in psychosis we make love
The love of the ageless, bottomless pit of time
As actors, we play out the scenes of a dream
For the moon is glorious in its reigning shine
But the beauty is in the moon's rising
Let us love one another in visions and dreams and imaginary scenes
As light cast upon the day is glorious and upon the night
Is a shining warm effervescent flow
For your arms wrapped all around me, is in the warmth of your wings

Woman

A woman is a delicate creature, the fruit of passion
The soft emotional fruit of sensitivity
A woman, like sweet berries, are plumped and with feeling
Like wine swirled and bubbly in your mouth
Woman! The romance is already in you
I just tip the glass and the juice runs out
All between your cleavage and down upon your bulging breast
Ladies look so attractive and romantic
As they drink the bubbly with the breath of
The effervescent esteemed wine, as it moves them
The ladies of proper principles, giggle as bubbly and refined sweet wine
So Ill bite into the fruit of their passions,
As sweet berries if squeezed, the juice runs out
"The darker the berry, the sweeter the wine!"
Naturally women are the darker berries in personality,
With a broader essence than a man
It's an experience to taste the intoxicating sweet wine of her emotions
To see a woman such a beautiful creature,
In many sorts of ways a man could never count
Ladies, you are as beautiful as you've always been, in a refined way
As age ripened wine, toasted and refined

A Beautiful Reflection

After a long day I walked up the stairs to my bedroom
To retire for the night
I opened a window to enjoy the cool summer night
I saw a light on next door and the shades were open wide
You could see the steam rising from the shower door
Then suddenly the door opened.
She walked out of the shower, in the nude
She reached for a shiny gold hair brush with long, soft bristles
She leaned over forward,
Flinging all her long brown hair over the top of her head
As her hair nearly touched the floor in front of her
She stroked her hair repeatedly,
Exposing her beautiful, wet crescent moon from behind
As the Mercury's rising, during the moment,
Imagining the taste of her sexual essence
After brushing her long soft brown hair,
She walked over to a full length mirror
Stared deeply into her reflection, as beauty stared back into her eyes
And she enjoyed her body as it feels sexy and erotic to her
Rubbing her hands down and around her perky breast
And loving the feeling of being a beautiful sexual creature, she smiled

Nightmare

Livid black rain, shadows and rivers of storms
Powered massive currents in dreams of heavy proportions
Graphic realizations and symbiotic frequencies, unnatural
And the parasitic dark essence damned eternal
The ramparts of eminent statured and cadesant towers
Mirages of empires and images from the times of the past
Suddenly, I awakened from that curse of a dream,
Somewhere between woke and sleep
I could see a dark image, in the eye of my mind that alerted me
I was frozen in a trance as the cold sweat streaked across my forehead
I felt the driving force of the dwellers, within the irony of the darkness
And the caricature of anger,
For the intensity of the madness frightened me
For they move between realms,
Fading into the blackness of satires in dreams
As I lay in bed unable to move,
In the dark bedroom with the door cracked open
I heard deep footsteps that sounded heavy by definition
Creeping sounds and imaginations flooded my mind
As I heard each foot step approach the dark bedroom
A cold stroke pierced through my beating heart
I sensed the zest of the moonlight and a monstrous dark shadow
A strange vile energy form, A violent essence and viciously wicked
As the dark image laid hold of the cracked door,
The room became charged with evil energy

I saw the light from the hallway enter into the dark bedroom
Slowly the door was creaking open, then suddenly the door stopped
I felt the rushing force of the wind,
Blow violently passed my face with great power and force of exertion
As the door shuddered completely wide open
The shine of the hallway light glared brightly behind
The tall darkened figure standing in the doorway
Stretching its arm toward the ceiling in a forty five degree angle
Then out stretched wings reached higher yet
As the monstrous entity began a vicious approach toward me
Giving off a grotesque foul odor
The electric charge of my heart beat plummeted to my feet
The entity attempted to come through a dream,
As if it were a portal into other dimensions
Precisely my reality was its course
As I traveled on a journey through my mind
I saw many aspects of my life, within a fraction of a second
Then in a moment, as clear as crystal, a great and powerful light
Vibrantly shining within the sky

An explosive blast of lightning and great thunder showering across the sky
As my heart skipped a beat, I sensed the power and command of the light
Vigilantly moving with excessive force, power, and glory
Great writings have been told concerning the light
As the light speedily flown across the sky,
Flying abruptly into the bedroom window
Vibrantly filling the room with light
And magnifying the power and the glory of the light
Swallowed up the darkness, as it vanished from the room
When the light left, the darkness was gone
I could feel the peace and joy at the same time,
But fell fast asleep as I drifted into slumber
In the morning, I awakened to a wide open door
Knowing fully well that I'd cracked the door
And turned out the lights before sleep

A Romantic Man

Proliferating verses resound through my mind
With original thoughts of love making
And profound transcending winds over matter
With the strength of my strong hands
And the firmness of my smooth gentle touch
As I speak to you in tender loving verses
of romantic interludes
And I touch you in all your sensitive places
Eruptions in the lower parts of your body
Explode into erotic dreams
And sexy imaginations in your mind
I control you with the passions
Lost deep within your soul
I have found new areas of erotica in your mind
I bring them out in you
And they're so satisfying to you

Absinthe in Dreams

An estate of a kingly domain
During the hours of darkness
In a point of time and of great pleasures
A world of brutish creatures
Touched by a virgin in delight
of fools and kings
As the seasons change
By the way of the night
My heart in flight rides upon the breeze
Far above the seas
And the Absinthe exudes
By the dopamine of aberrations in dreams
Of green fairies in my sight
And spoken vernacular
Of higher things seen as vapors
Dissipating steam dissolves into dreams
So tranquil and serene

America's Third World

Censorship in America's land
The freedom clocks have stopped in real time
Living machines activated
The states succumbed, slavery afoot!
And new age ethics subdue the land
The moral mines explode
Think tank time machine brings war to the free lands
The love of money rules the people's minds, under control
Living in a tank of virtual worlds, locked out of reality
Feeding on the imaginary lives, a downloaded existence
And continuation of starvation in American dreams, lost up to date
The city of Angels is fallen
The Statue of Liberty in American laws is gone
Dumbing down the people
The ruler of the land is the authority in the air
And the God of this world will not prevail

Particle Collider

Operating within natural zones of time
A powering juggernaut performs
As a key to unlock the door of time
Weakened shields of the Earth's dynamo
magneto sphere dissipation
Energy forms in high concentration
Electrical lightning transfer subtle
warnings from worldly powers
National discharges mitigate fluctuating color
changes all within the sky
Mega overload structure collapse
Transistors of pyramids energy ions emits currents
And magnetic fields show
Negative orientation projection patterns
Several large bodies, abrupt shifting storms
Gamma ray burst, black hole trajectories changed
Harnessed energy captured high constants
Open portals connecting time and eternal consequences formed

The Scope of the Human Mind

People base belief on what is perceived
to be seen within their mind
If people never experience
particular situations or instances,
They never have belief.
To see physically or mental images in the mind subjectively
Is why people began to believe
As shadows unseen, distort visual perception
Viewed tangible images imaginations,
occupied building blocks of protons
Formed realizations in physical realities
According to the material of matter
The creation of existence take form
Neutrons and protons experienced in the physical realm
Or seen within the scope of imagination
Bringing thoughts to realization and reality

Shining Forth

Your palatable adorability shines forth
From your covering as skin all over your body
Being a vein of existence, energetic waves
And vibes of electric energy
I adore your whole being, body, soul, and mind
A sculpture in abstract forms
The casting of realities essence
A silent choir, visually broadcast
Carved incisively penetrating to acute degrees
Analytically discerning as it shines forth the trials of this world
And tribulations of different subtle shapes,
colors, and expressions known

The Light within the Darkness

And seeing through the eyes of my mind
A war zone of imagination
Fading into obscurity of the twilight's soft glowing lights
Still able to see within the essence of the dawn, tantalizing light!
All around me, and about me, surrounding me
In the diffused dark space of the northern hemisphere light
But the symbiotic parasite within the darkness of anchored spirits
Reserved shadows and fulfilled black saturations reaching beyond
The tumult plateau of dark dreams in the night
And lower channels within dark places
For the light is merely a foreshadow of what is yet to come
Hallelujah, the light will increase abundantly!
And soon, there will be no night

Time and Space

To smell the rain in the moist, dense air is refreshing
Amidst the rolling thunder before the rain drops fall
Darkness lays as sack cloth across the lands
The hourglass turns within the motion sands
Moments fly, the visual sands of time
As the wind blows and the pendulum chimes
From whence the wind blows and speedily it goes
As never you'll know from whence you go
It's all the same from whence you came
Away from the land of time,
out into eternity past and future space
No effect of time or the vastness in space

Time Travel

The emergent essences of my body retracts from its existence
Moving into a traveling mode of flight
Experiencing many facets of life realities
The personification of the life force of living beings
Traveled in transient fleeting ephemeral motions short lived
And essence gained emphatically by illusions of effects
Perceived within my own repertoire
A man out of place and position
Living in a different time and place
Of which reality belongs to another genre in existence

Words are Powerful and Eternal

Poetry is shaping the clay with natural and conforming hands
In essence of a mold within the mind expressed
A bridge into the actuality sphere of
Unusual, bizarre, sky colored, dark vines of green
The essence of inevitable pathways
The ties that bind us together
For the password to your heart
Contracts not written or spoken but felt
For your heart, the abstract extension of expression
The materialized countenance of your face
Spoken words cut the wind, slicing the air in force
The diagrams of communications flow critically in thought
Engaging energies, benign through her painted lips
Words take off with magnificent wings
Keeping me locked inside ones heart

The Woman Within The Room

I entered a dim lighted room
Sat down onto a wooden chair
I saw a woman there, from inside the room
She was wearing a beautiful, red mini skirt
And sexy wedged heel shoes on her feet
She entered the room and sat down in a chair
I could see the essence of fantasy in her eyes
And the passionate dreamy expression on her face,
Melted me like butter
As she began to clear her throat quietly
In lieu of her mind being full of sexy secret passions
As the bottom of her short mini skirt
Slides up gently upon the inner middle of her silky thighs
And crossing her legs as she rubbed her tender silky thighs together firmly
Bringing her moist walls of affection together for erotic stimulation
As she sits in the chair in the darkened room

Infidelity

Romance cannot exist in the prism of infidelity
Fragrant affairs lead to busy lives and scares
Always before a relationship we see the bright side of others
But as soon as the commitment takes hold
The darkness of a crown of diadems sets into the fold

Exotic Perfume

She was well fragranced with the aroma of the vanilla bean
As exotic as it may seem but it was the sight of her sexy silhouette
A profile of perfection that attracted me
Her eyes shine like new money with the jingle of the coin
Her breath was as crisp as a brand new paper dollar bill
Smelling good with exotic oils and perfume
She was always so clean all the way through
And most of all in between
So I'll never use a cover when we make love
Because natural is by far above

Ebony and Ivory

She complemented me while enjoying the dark chocolate roast
And the fine caramel color of my beautiful, black skin
She compared her porcelain white skin to mine
She was excited and very much turned on
She told me how she oozed in heat
For the forbidden essence of the blackness of my dark skin
The essence of ebony and ivory created a conundrum in our minds
But the urge of the passion was too great
The mere thought of black and white gently slamming together
In a wet pool of familiar juices, like the motion of a potion
As the wet erotica turned us both on
The venom within our minds was the passion we most hoped for
Colorfully so, in darker shades of gray
She loved the mysteriousness of my blackness
And her pale nude body turned me on
And her beautiful heart shaped posterior
Was like the still light of a pale moon
She enjoyed black love because the cocktail
I delivered was so intoxicating
She could barely walk after we made love
The lower region of my body was just the right proportion
As it was fitting as the perfect key inside a lock
To open, the door wide

Beautiful Senorita

Oh my senorita, what a beautiful specimen,
What a gorgeous Spanish fly whistling within the sky
And flying amidst the thickets of the clouds.
Everything about this woman is more than original.
The flare of her hair, the bounce of her breast when she walks;
And the beauty and curvature of her derriere,
Is so divine and flowing when she moves.
For the Nair removes the hair, from her sexy brown legs.
And the way that beautiful lace bra fits to form
Around her firm bulging breasts.
Even more you can see her sexy panties,
Through that beautiful red dress
And I love the way that string, fits between her seam.
She's a beautiful taco salad, with flaming hot taco sauce,
A deep fried taco shell, packing lots of goodies inside.
I would like to put that scenario on the table,
And when I am done eating, I am going to lick the plate.
A trick and a treat.
She is sweet and sour to her feet,
Like a margarita with sugar on the rim and cool,
But not a fool.

Elite

They lust for control and power, eternal.
They twist the minds of the people that follow them tight.
Lacking the source of light and sight, working under their own might!
They strive as a beehive in reprieve buzzing through life instinctual,
And not right.
Against the people swarming bees, they bumble, sting and bite.
They're elite and they fight but at the end of the day, they're never right.
They shuck and jive on a quest to stay alive.
But for you, they thrill and have the will to kill.
On the eve of the hour, the season of the times,
Is closely at the end of the days.

Hollywood Actors

All within the prism of Hollywood's Kabbalah,
The actors, mellow dramas and bipartisan characters.
The favors and flavors
The plays and the roles of the opera
The roles with the same goals
Fleeting paths, as they go along their merry palms weary travelers way.
Navigating the reeds ways foliage scape upon secret lives,
Casted spells, eerie smells and the roses which lie beneath their noses.
For its real, it can kill when you sign upon that dotted line.
For the broth in this soup, is not even for a soup at all,
But Empirical spirits that mold into the plane
Of our environment undetected.
Mirroring our thoughts for deceptions quasi seducing forms,
That blend, unseen into this plane of the third dimension.

TERRELL W. SIMS
Autobiography

My name is Terrell W. Sims and I was born on the 5th of September, 1965 in Wichita, Kansas. My parents are Eugene Sims and Josephine Sims. My early childhood was a normal lower middle class environment in the 60s and 70s. I had four sisters and two brothers. My dad ran his own lawn care service and my mom was a stay at home mother. I graduated from Wichita East High in 1984. I completed some college at Wichita State University and started in the work world. I met my wife, Azadeh Sims and married on October 17th of 1995. We have a son and he is our only child and is now 25 years old and out of the nest. I started writing poetry in 2007 as a hobby and a way to express my emotions, feelings and thoughts.

www.ingramcontent.com/pod-product-compliance
Lightning Source LLC
Chambersburg PA
CBHW031223120626
46545CB00003B/958